Copyright © 2017 by Calpine Memory Books
All rights reserved. This book or any portion thereof
may not be reproduced or used in any manner whatsoever
without the express written permission of the publisher.

THE GUEST BOOK OF

_____

_____

Guest Names: _____

Dates of Visit: _____

Traveling From: _____

Favorite Memories From Visit:

_____

_____

_____

_____

Things I Would Recommend:

_____

_____

_____

_____

Guest Names: _____

Dates of Visit: _____

Traveling From: _____

Favorite Memories From Visit:

_____
_____
_____
_____

Things I Would Recommend:

_____
_____
_____
_____

Guest Names: _____

Dates of Visit: _____

Traveling From: _____

Favorite Memories From Visit:

_____
_____
_____
_____
_____

Things I Would Recommend:

_____
_____
_____
_____

Guest Names: _____

Dates of Visit: _____

Traveling From: _____

Favorite Memories From Visit:

_____

_____

_____

_____

Things I Would Recommend:

_____

_____

_____

_____

Guest Names: _____

Dates of Visit: _____

Traveling From: _____

Favorite Memories From Visit:

_____
_____
_____
_____

Things I Would Recommend:

_____
_____
_____

Guest Names: _____

Dates of Visit: _____

Traveling From: _____

Favorite Memories From Visit:

_____

_____

_____

_____

_____

Things I Would Recommend:

_____

_____

_____

_____

Guest Names: _____

Dates of Visit: _____

Traveling From: _____

Favorite Memories From Visit:

_____
_____
_____
_____

Things I Would Recommend:

_____
_____
_____
_____

Guest Names: _____

Dates of Visit: _____

Traveling From: _____

Favorite Memories From Visit:

_____

_____

_____

_____

Things I Would Recommend:

_____

_____

_____

_____

Guest Names: _____

Dates of Visit: _____

Traveling From: _____

Favorite Memories From Visit:

_____
_____
_____
_____

Things I Would Recommend:

_____
_____
_____

Guest Names: _____

Dates of Visit: _____

Traveling From: _____

Favorite Memories From Visit:

_____

_____

_____

_____

_____

Things I Would Recommend:

_____

_____

_____

_____

Guest Names: _____

Dates of Visit: _____

Traveling From: _____

Favorite Memories From Visit:

_____

_____

_____

_____

_____

Things I Would Recommend:

_____

_____

_____

_____

Guest Names: _____

Dates of Visit: _____

Traveling From: _____

Favorite Memories From Visit:

_____
_____
_____
_____

Things I Would Recommend:

_____
_____
_____
_____

Guest Names: _____

Dates of Visit: _____

Traveling From: _____

Favorite Memories From Visit:

_____

_____

_____

_____

_____

Things I Would Recommend:

_____

_____

_____

_____

Guest Names: _____

Dates of Visit: _____

Traveling From: _____

Favorite Memories From Visit:

_____

_____

_____

_____

Things I Would Recommend:

_____

_____

_____

_____

Guest Names: _____

Dates of Visit: _____

Traveling From: _____

Favorite Memories From Visit:

_____

_____

_____

_____

Things I Would Recommend:

_____

_____

_____

_____

Guest Names: _____

Dates of Visit: _____

Traveling From: _____

Favorite Memories From Visit:

_____
_____
_____
_____
_____

Things I Would Recommend:

_____
_____
_____
_____

Guest Names: _____

Dates of Visit: _____

Traveling From: _____

Favorite Memories From Visit:

_____

_____

_____

_____

Things I Would Recommend:

_____

_____

_____

_____

Guest Names: _____

Dates of Visit: _____

Traveling From: _____

Favorite Memories From Visit:

_____
_____
_____
_____

Things I Would Recommend:

_____
_____
_____
_____

Guest Names: _____

Dates of Visit: _____

Traveling From: _____

Favorite Memories From Visit:

_____
_____
_____
_____
_____

Things I Would Recommend:

_____
_____
_____
_____

Guest Names: _____

Dates of Visit: _____

Traveling From: _____

Favorite Memories From Visit:

_____
_____
_____
_____
_____

Things I Would Recommend:

_____
_____
_____
_____

Guest Names: _____

Dates of Visit: _____

Traveling From: _____

Favorite Memories From Visit:

_____

_____

_____

_____

Things I Would Recommend:

_____

_____

_____

_____

Guest Names: _____

Dates of Visit: _____

Traveling From: _____

Favorite Memories From Visit:

_____
_____
_____
_____

Things I Would Recommend:

_____
_____
_____

Guest Names: _____

Dates of Visit: _____

Traveling From: _____

Favorite Memories From Visit:

_____
_____
_____
_____

Things I Would Recommend:

_____
_____
_____

Guest Names: _____

Dates of Visit: _____

Traveling From: _____

Favorite Memories From Visit:

_____

_____

_____

_____

Things I Would Recommend:

_____

_____

_____

_____

Guest Names: _____

Dates of Visit: _____

Traveling From: _____

Favorite Memories From Visit:

_____
_____
_____
_____

Things I Would Recommend:

_____
_____
_____
_____

Printed in Great Britain
by Amazon